T0171675

PRAISE FOR *AFTER NATURE*

"Before the four incomparable novels that made him a world figure in literature, W. G. Sebald wrote the free verse triptych *After Nature*, now fluently translated by Michael Hamburger. *After Nature* sets the pattern of the novels: reveries on distant lives alongside something like autobiography. This and the later books sustain a search for threads along which conscious and lost memories in private life connect with surviving and lost evidence about lives and worlds long gone. . . . As in Sebald's novels, images and echoes link narrative meditations in this work."   —*The San Francisco Chronicle*

"[There are] three poems in *After Nature*. The first is about the sixteenth-century painter Matthias Grünewald, the second about the nineteenth-century botanist Georg Steller, [and the third] is an autobiographical prose poem. The scientist, the artist, and the writer all trying to make sense of life and death, pulled between images of white snow in the Alps and green forests and pastures. The late W. G. Sebald is a writer who often stops, in his quest for meaning, with the unexplained coincidence. [Sebald] will not translate coincidence for his readers, and this is the secret of his perfect timing. Here is the other secret: We are willing to be carried along in a haze of not quite understanding because Sebald also revels in the pure music of words. . . . Only by suspending readerly willfulness will you be able to float weightless through his writing."   —*Los Angeles Times*

"Remarkably lucid English translation . . . *After Nature* consists of three interrelated narratives, spanning different historical periods. . . . It is Sebald's graphic description of a subject in a Grünewald painting that seems to capture the random, irrational movements of nature most vividly."
—*The Washington Post*

"Europe . . . is a continent soaked in bloody history; its every street corner, its every green and lovely field has likely borne witness to some episode of war or religious terror or plague. W. G. Sebald . . . was a master at evoking this haunted Europe. . . . By the time he died on a rural English road, he had been acknowledged as one of the great postwar European writers. . . . Now, *After Nature*, a book of three long poems by Sebald, is being published in

English for the first time. . . . This translation (by his friend Michael Hamburger) reveals him to be a poet of subtlety and lingering power."

—*Time Out New York*

"His work recalls Gustav Herling's *Journal Written at Night* or, when he includes uncaptioned photographs, the early work of Sebald's contemporary, Michael Ondaatje. Comparisons, however, do no justice to Sebald. Eventually, even the most familiar prose unit, the paragraph, dissolves in his hands. He was an original." —*The Philadelphia Inquirer*

"The three long poems in *After Nature* . . . anatomize the correspondence between the life and the work, the work and the world, the world and the life. Wary of abstraction, alert to history's detours and infernal turns, Sebald had the ability to consort with the unspeakable. . . . *After Nature* is Sebald's alpha and omega, at once the first and last of his literary works, and a seedbed for his later projects. . . . Sebald, near the end of *After Nature*, under a lowering sky, writes, 'What's dead is gone/forever,' then a shard from Lear: 'What did'st /thou say?' More questions follow, and the section dissolves into 'Water? Fire? Good?/Evil? Life? Death?' It's the one moment in his entire body of work where he gives the impression of losing control, and the effect is liberating and haunting." —*The Village Voice*

"The art that he created is of near-miraculous beauty."

—*The New Republic*

"*After Nature*, which now appears in an excellent translation by Michael Hamburger, is a work of considerable scope and ambition. . . . The aims of the Grünewald and Steller poems are not biographical or historical in any ordinary sense. Though the scholarship behind them is thorough . . . scholarship takes second place to what he intuits about his subjects and perhaps projects upon them. . . . It is thus best to think of Grünewald and Steller as personae, masks that enable Sebald to project back into the past a character type, ill at ease in the world, indeed in exile from it, that may be his own but that he feels possesses a certain genealogy which his reading and researches can uncover. . . . 'Dark Night Sallies Forth,' the third of the poems in *After Nature*, is more overtly autobiographical. Here, Sebald, as 'I,' takes stock of himself as a person but also as inheritor of Germany's recent history."

—*The New York Review of Books*

AFTER NATURE

AFTER NATURE

W. G. Sebald

Translated from the German by
Michael Hamburger

THE MODERN LIBRARY
NEW YORK

LIBRARY OF CONGRESS CATALOGING-IN-PUBLICATION DATA
Sebald, Winfried Georg, 1944–2001
[Nach der Natur. English]
After nature / W. G. Sebald.—1st ed.
p.   cm.
ISBN 978-0-375-75658-0
I. Title.
PT2681.E18N3313   2002
833'.914—dc21

147429898

...AS THE SNOW ON THE ALPS

Or va, ch'un sol volere è d'ambedue:
tu duca, tu segnore e tu maestro.
Così li dissi; e poi che mosso fue,
intrai per lo cammino alto e silvestro.

Now go, the will within us being one:
you be my guide, Lord, master from this day,
I said to him; and when he, moved, led on
I entered on the steep wild-wooded way.

Dante, *Inferno,* Canto II

··· I ···

Whoever closes the wings
of the altar in the Lindenhardt
parish church and locks up
the carved figures in their casing
on the lefthand panel
will be met by St. George.
Foremost at the picture's edge he stands
above the world by a hand's breadth
and is about to step over the frame's
threshold. Georgius Miles,
man with the iron torso, rounded chest
of ore, red-golden hair and silver
feminine features. The face of the unknown
Grünewald emerges again and again
in his work as a witness
to the snow miracle, a hermit
in the desert, a commiserator
in the Munich *Mocking of Christ*.

Last of all, in the afternoon light
in the Erlangen library, it shines forth
from a self-portrait, sketched out
in heightened white crayon, later destroyed
by an alien hand's pen and wash,
as that of a painter aged forty
to fifty. Always the same
gentleness, the same burden of grief,
the same irregularity of the eyes, veiled
and sliding sideways down into loneliness.
Grünewald's face reappears, too,
in a Basel painting by Holbein
the Younger of a crowned female saint.
These were strangely disguised
instances of resemblance, wrote Fraenger
whose books were burned by the fascists.
Indeed it seemed as though in such works of art
men had revered each other like brothers, and
often made monuments in each other's
image where their paths had crossed.
Hence too, at the centre of
the Lindenhardt altar's right wing,
that troubled gaze upon the youth
on the other side of the older man
whom, years ago now, on a grey
January morning I myself once

encountered in the railway station
in Bamberg. It is St. Dionysius,
his cut-off head under one arm.
To him, his chosen guardian
who in the midst of life carries
his death with him, Grünewald gives
the appearance of Riemenschneider, whom
twenty years later the Würzburg bishop
condemned to the breaking of his hands
in the torture cell. Long before that time
pain had entered into the pictures.
That is the command, knows the painter
who on the altar aligns himself
with the scant company of the
fourteen auxiliary saints. Each of these,
the blessed Blasius, Achaz and Eustace;
Panthaleon, Aegidius, Cyriax, Christopher and
Erasmus and the truly beautiful
St. Vitus with the cockerel,
each look in different
directions without knowing
why. The three female saints
Barbara, Catherine and Margaret on
the other hand hide at the edge
of the left panel behind the back of
St. George putting together their

uniform oriental heads for
a conspiracy against the men.
The misfortune of saints
is their sex, is the terrible
separation of the sexes which Grünewald
suffered in his own person. The exorcised
devil that Cyriax, not only because
of the narrow confines, holds raised
high as an emblem in
the air is a female being
and, as a grisaille of Grünewald's
in the Frankfurt Städel shows in
the most drastic of fashions, derives from
Diocletian's epileptic daughter,
the misshapen princess Artemia whom
Cyriax, as beside him she kneels on
the ground, holds tightly leashed
with a maniple of his vestments
like a dog. Spreading out
above them is the branch work
of a fig tree with fruit, one of which
is entirely hollowed out by insects.

···II···

Little is known of the life of
Matthaeus Grünewald of Aschaffenburg.
The first account of the painter
in Joachim von Sandrart's *German Academy*
of the year 1675 begins with the notice
that the author knows not one person living
who could provide a written or oral
testimony of that praiseworthy hand.
We may trust that report by Sandrart,
for a portrait in a Würzburg museum
has preserved him, aged eighty-two,
wide awake and with eyes uncommonly clear.
Lightly in grey and black,
he writes, Matthaeus had painted the outer
wings of an altarpiece made by Dürer
of Mary's ascension in the
Preachers' convent in Frankfurt and
thus had lived at around 1505.

Exceedingly strange was the trans-
figuration of Christ on Mount Tabor
limned by him in watercolours, especially
one cloud of wondrous beauty, wherein
above the Apostles convulsed
with awe, Moses and Elijah appear,
a marvel surpassed.
Then in the Mainz cathedral
there had been three altar panels
with facing fronts and reverse
sides painted, one of them
showing a blind hermit who, as he crosses
the frozen Rhine river with a boy
to guide him, is assaulted by two murderers
and beaten to death. Anno 1631 or '32,
this panel in the wild war of that era
had been taken away and sent off to Sweden
but by shipwreck beside many other
such pieces of art had perished
in the depths of the sea.
At Isenheim, Sandrart had not been,
but had heard of the altar-work there,
which, he writes, was so fashioned that
real life could scarce have been other
and where, it was said, a *St. Anthony* with
demons meticulously drawn was to be seen.

Except for a *St. John* with hands clasped
of which he, Sandrart, when at one time in Rome
he was counterfeiting the pope, had caught sight,
with certainty this was all that was not lost
of the work of the Aschaffenburg
painter of whom, besides, he knew only
that most of the time he had
resided in Mainz, led a reclusive
melancholy life and been ill-married.

We know there is a long tradition
of persecuting the Jews, in the City
of Frankfurt as in other places.
Around 1240, the records tell us,
173 were either slaughtered
or died of their own free will
in a conflagration. In 1349
the Flagellant Brothers instituted
a great massacre in the Jewish quarter.
Again, the chronicles tell that the Jews
burned themselves and that
after the fire there was a clear view from
the Cathedral Hill over to Sachsenhausen.
Thereafter the Jews only hesitantly
returned to the city on the Main.
In the mid–fifteenth century
a clothing statute is issued,
yellow rings to be worn on the tunic,

later a grey circle the size of
an apple, for the prevention of all
carnal intercourse between Christians
and Jews, for a long time to come
under the pain of death.
Then, at the expense of Frankfurt's
high city council, in the train
of civic reform, progressive order
and hygienisation, a ghetto of their own
is built for the Jews by the Wollgraben,
fourteen houses and a new synagogue.
By Grünewald's time, we learn,
there are twenty-three houses, and soon
the district counts more than three thousand souls
without the boundaries having been widened.
Each night—on Sundays at four in the
afternoon—they were locked up, and
might not walk into any place
where a green tree grew,
not on the Scheidewall
nor in the Ross, nor on the Römerberg
or in the Avenue. In this ghetto
the Jewess Enchin had been raised
before, not many months preceding
her marriage to Mathys Grune
the painter, she was christened

in the name of St. Anne.

In the compendious book about the historical
Grünewald which Dr. W. K. Zülch produced
in ancient Schwabach type,
in the year 1938 for Hitler's birthday
the story of this extraordinary union
could not be admitted. Grünewald
would have noticed this child,
remarkable, it was said, for her beauty
when she passed through the Bridge Gate
and the Preachers' Lane on her way
to her workplace just outside the ghetto.
But there is no evidence that it was he who induced
this Anna, betrothed to him a year later,
to change her religious faith.
Rather it seems that she herself
had facilitated this step
attesting great strength of will,
or desperation, by looking the painter
straight in the eyes; perhaps
at first merely in love with
his green-colored name,
a conjunction which to the bachelor
master, who meanwhile had given up
the Mainz Court Painter's appointment
in favour of the great Isenheim Altar

commission, will not have come amiss,
for without a household of his own
he could employ no assistant
or apprentice for his work.
When Grünewald buys a house
very close to the cathedral
on December 17th 1512
for twenty-three guilders
twelve shillings, already,
the documents record, he has taken
to wife the baptised Anna.
The much admired young proselyte,
who for the Frankfurt Christian
community, which even for her baptism
had overwhelmed her with gifts,
was no mean acquisition, and
could have founded Grünewald's fortune.
If it fell out otherwise, for one thing
it was because the painter
who later lived as a recluse
and almost underground, himself
made impossible his recognition
by this community; and,
for another, as his pictures prove,
he had more of an eye for men,
whose faces and entire physique

he executed with endless devotion
whereas his women for the most part
are veiled, so relieving him of the fear
of looking at them more closely.
Perhaps that is why Grünewald's
Anna grew shrewish, ill, a victim
to perverse reason, to brain fevers
and to madness.
In the end, awaiting recovery,
she is placed in hospital where
at the time of the painter's death
still she lives on, infirm
in body and mind.

··· IV ···

In the Chicago Art Institute
hangs the self-portrait of an unknown
young painter which in 1929
passed into the Frankfurt art trade
from Sweden. The small maple panel
shows a scarcely twenty-year-old
at the window of a narrow room.
Behind him, on a shelf not quite
in perspective, pots of paint,
a crayon, a seashell and a precious Venetian
glass filled with a translucent essence.
In one hand the painter holds
a finely carved knife of bone
with which to trim the drawing-pen
before continuing work on a female nude
that lies in front of him next to an inkwell.
Through the window on his left a
landscape with mountain and valley

and the curved line of a path is visible.
This last, Zülch philosophises, is the way
into the world, and no one took it other
than the man, vanished without a trace,
to whom his research is devoted and whose art
he thinks he can recognise in the anonymous picture.
The reason for the signature "M.N."
above the window-frame must be
that the painter Mathis Nithart,
discovered in archives but otherwise
not identified by any works of his own,
hid behind the name of Grünewald.
Hence the initials M.G. and N. on the Snow
Altar at Aschaffenburg, hence the merging,
most remarkable, given the difference in age,
of the young painter with the Sebastian
pierced with arrows at Isenheim.
And indeed the person of Mathis Nithart
in documents of the time so flows into
the person of Grünewald that one
seems to have been the life,
then the death, too, of the other.
An X-ray photograph of the Sebastian panel
reveals beneath the elegiac
portrait of the saint
that same face again, the half-

profile only turned a tiny bit further
in the definitive overpainting.
Here two painters in one body
whose hurt flesh belonged to both
to the end pursued the study
of their own nature. At first
Nithart fashioned his self-portrait
from a mirror image, and Grünewald
with great love, precision and patience
and an interest in the skin
and hair of his companion extending
to the blue shadow of the beard
then overpainted it.
The martyrdom depicted is
the representation, to be sensed
even in the rims of the wounds,
of a male friendship wavering
between horror and loyalty.
It is conceivable that Nithart
who was also a maker of water displays,
in later years furthered
the mistaking of his person for
the increasingly unsociable Isenheim master,
that perhaps he was the connecting link
between Grünewald and the world become
inaccessible to him in his misfortune.

Around 1527, about twelve
years after the work in Alsace,
Nithart moved from Frankfurt, where
for a time he must have continued to share
the life of Grünewald, to Halle
to build, for its celebrated salt springs,
watercourses and an array
of jet fountains driven
by a most complicated system of scoop
wheels and pipes like that on the Main
at Aschaffenburg, a masterpiece of
mechanical art much visited at the time.
It is said, however, that Nithart
never accomplished much in Halle and often
changed lodgings. In the summer of
'twenty-eight he fell into
deep dejection and then, it seems,
death very soon overtook him.
The Frankfurt magistrates, when the news
of Nithart's passing had reached them,
ordered a register to be made
of the household effects in his
workshop. The long list embraces
an accumulation of the most diverse things:
spoons and pottage bowls, soup cauldrons,
drawing-belts for water, fifteen

white goatskins, silver talers,
and copper coins from Schwaz in the Tyrol,
books, proclamations, scripts and many
Lutheran printed tracts. All this
irradiated by the glory of a unique
store of paints: lead white and albus,
Paris red, cinnabar, slate green,
mountain green, alchemy green, blue
vitreous pastes and minerals
from the Orient. Clothing, too,
beautiful, *item* a gold-yellow pair of hose,
tunics, cinnamon-coloured, the lapels overlaid
in purpled velvet with black stitching,
a grey atlas doublet, a red slouch hat
and much exquisite adornment besides.
The estate in truth is that of two men, but
whether Grünewald, an inventor of singular
hues, shared his departed friend's liking
for such gaudy arrayment
we cannot presume to say.

· · · V · · ·

At the point where the great military road
from Strasbourg to the Burgundian portal, in line with
the run of the Vosges to the south,
crosses the Lauterbach's course
from the Gebweiler transverse valley,
lies the village of Isenheim.
Here the Canons Regular,
the legendary history of whose order
is traced back to the anchorite
Antonius the Hermit who
in the year 357 departed this life
in the Theban desert, in 1300
acquired the site from the Murbach
Cluniacs to found an Antonian hospital
for the cure of St. Anthony's fire
which raged throughout all Europe,
an infection of the blood that led
to the rotting away of the limbs

and with leprosy was among
the most dreaded diseases of the Middle Ages.
When gradually St. Anthony's fire
died, the Antonian hospitals adopted
other ailments that afflicted body or mind
for their healing, such as epilepsy
and the so-called venereal scourges
which spread disastrously after 1490.
The treatment of patients who at their arrival
were usually half-destroyed already
tended towards this, that, as
hieratic witnesses to evil,
at first they were led to the altar
in the choir aisle, baptised in the name
of a martyr to God and so, as it were
despite and together with their perversion,
brought into the precincts of salvation.
In this it happened not infrequently
that from the relic of St. Anthony
encased in the shrine of the altar
a miracle emanated, or that
those in some part horribly disfigured were
later rid of their affliction by the repeated
application of *Saint Vinage,* an elixir
which the canons obtained annually
on the day of the Resurrection in the monastery

of St. Antoine de Viennois,
near St. Marcellin on the Isère
by pouring wine on the bones,
there preserved, of St. Anthony.
This liquid, twice purified,
was distributed by the monastery's messengers
up and down the country, and with it
the peasants blessed that pig which
in their sties wore the bell of the saint,
who was also the patron of flocks and their keepers.
As for the hospital itself, where
of the twelve canons eight
usually studied philosophy
under a lector,
the rituals of purification
according to which the sick were treated
became a battle fought over their bodies
against the presence of death manifested
in madness; became indeed the most
fundamental of all confrontations
in which the altar-work commissioned
from Grünewald by Guido Guersi,
the Isenheim Preceptor, was to engage
the painter in a great therapeutic
task through the representation,
executed in beauteous and harrowing

colours, of the hour of the pale
streams of pus. At the latest
with the commencement of his work
in the Alsatian Home of the Crippled
where the most diverse material for inspection
of the manners in which a human being
creeps into himself, herself or
seeks to get out, was assembled,
Grünewald, who in any case must have tended
towards an extremist view of the world,
will have come to see the redemption of the
living as one from life itself.
Now life as such, as it unfolds, dreadfully,
everywhere and at all times,
is not to be seen on the altar panels
whose figures have passed beyond
the miseries of existence, unless it be
in that unreal and demented thronging
which Grünewald has developed around
St. Anthony of the temptation:
dragged by his hair over the ground
by a gruesome monster.
Low down in the bottom-left corner
cowers the body, covered with
syphilitic chancres, of an inmate
of the Isenheim hospital. Above it

rises a two-headed and many-
armed androgynous creature
about to finish off the saint
with a brandished jaw-bone.
On the right, a stilt-legged bird-like beast
which, with human arms,
holds a cudgel raised up. Behind
and beside this, towards the picture's centre,
crab-clawed together, shark- and dragon-like
maws, rows of teeth, pug noses
from which snot flows, fin-shaped
clammy limp wings, hair and horns,
skin like entrails turned outwards,
excrescences of an entire life,
in the air, on land and in water.
To him, the painter, this is creation,
image of our insane presence
on the surface of the earth,
the regeneration proceeding
in downward orbits
whose parasitical shapes
intertwine, and, growing into
and out of one another, surge
as a demonic swarm
into the hermit's quietude.
In this fashion Grünewald,

silently wielding his paintbrush,
rendered the scream, the wailing, the gurgling
and the shrieking of a pathological spectacle
to which he and his art, as he must have known,
themselves belong. The panic-stricken
kink in the neck to be seen
in all of Grünewald's subjects,
exposing the throat and often turning
the face towards a blinding light,
is the extreme response of our bodies
to the absence of balance in nature
which blindly makes one experiment after another
and like a senseless botcher
undoes the thing it has only just achieved.
To try out how far it can go
is the sole aim of this sprouting,
perpetuation and proliferation
inside us also and through us and through
the machines sprung from our heads,
all in a single jumble,
while behind us already the green
trees are leaving their leaves and
bare, as often they appear in Grünewald's
pictures, loom up into the sky,
the dead branches overlaid
with a moss-like glutinous substance.

The black bird that in its beak
carries a break-time meal
to St. Anthony on his site
in the desert may be the one with
the heart of glass, the bird
flying ever closer to us,
of which another prophet
of the last days announces
that it will shit into the sea
so that the water boils itself out,
that the earth trembles and the great city
with the iron tower stands in flames,
whilst the Pope squats in a barge
and darkness comes and
with it a yellow dust
that covers the land.

··· VI ···

On the Basel *Crucifixion* of 1505
behind the group of mourners
a landscape reaches so far into the depth
that our eyes cannot see its limits.
A patch of brown scorched earth
whose contour like the head of a whale
or an open-mouthed leviathan
devours the pale green meadow plains,
and the marshily shining stretches
of water. Above it, pushed off
to behind the horizon, which step
by step grows darker, more glowering,
rise the hills of the prehistory
of the Passion. We see the gate
of the Garden of Gethsemane, the approach
of the henchmen and the kneeling figure of Christ
so reduced in size that in the
receding space the rushing

away of time can be sensed.
Most probably Grünewald painted
and recalled the catastrophic incursion
of darkness, the last trace of light
flickering from beyond, after nature,
for in the year 1502, when he was working
at Bindlach, below the Fichtelgebirge,
on the creation of the Lindenhardt altar,
on the first of October the moon's shadow
slid over Eastern Europe from Mecklenburg
over Bohemia and the Lausitz to southern Poland,
and Grünewald, who repeatedly was in touch
with the Aschaffenburg Court Astrologer Johann Indagine,
will have travelled to see this event of the century,
awaited with great terror, the eclipse of the sun,
so will have become a witness to
the secret sickening away of the world,
in which a phantasmal encroachment of dusk
in the midst of daytime like a fainting fit
poured through the vault of the sky,
while over the banks of mist and the cold
heavy blues of the clouds
a fiery red arose, and colours
such as his eyes had not known
radiantly wandered about, never again to be
driven out of the painter's memory.

These colours unfold as the reverse of
the spectrum in a different consistency
of the air, whose deoxygenated void
in the gasping breath of the figures
on the central Isenheim panel is enough
to portend our death by asphyxiation; after which
comes the mountain landscape of weeping
in which Grünewald with a pathetic gaze
into the future has prefigured
a planet utterly strange, chalk-coloured
behind the blackish-blue river.
Here in an evil state of erosion
and desolation the heritage of the ruining
of life that in the end will consume
even the stones has been depicted.
In view of this it seems to me
that the ice age, the glaringly white
towering of the summits in
the upper realm of the *Temptation,*
is the construction of a metaphysic
and a miracle like the one
in the year 352, when
at the height of the summer
snow fell
on the Esquiline
Hill in Rome.

···VII···

In the spring of 1525 Grünewald
rode through April light and showers
to Windsheim, where from the workshop
of Jakob Seckler he had ordered
the crowning piece for an altar,
an intricate carving of finials
and figures, vine leaves and
various birds. While Seckler
put the last touch to his work,
Grünewald fell into conversation
with Barthel and Sebald Beham,
etchers and draughtsmen from Nürnberg who,
seized on January 12th as godless painters
and driven out of their native city for heresy,
were lodging provisionally at the Windsheim master's.
The brothers, on walks out into the still
discoloured fields and till late into the night,
told of Thomas Münzer, at one time in Nürnberg,

now gone through Swabia to Alsace,
to Switzerland and into the Black Forest
to raise the insurrection. For the sixth
trumpet was about to sound and the poor
letter must be released from its prison.
With clangour a great
pentecost was to begin,
the filling of the waters well nigh
completed, the seething
planets gathered in
the house of Pisces. The red
star was drawing into conjunction
with Saturn, the sign
of the peasants, and a fantastic
fire would flare up when,
in the imminent future,
a needy wretch would be revealed
as the Messiah Septentrionalis.
Grünewald said that once, in his childhood,
he must have been six or seven,
the kettle drummer of Niklashausen
had roused the people with promises
of earthly happiness for the poor.
Fifty thousand daily had thronged to him,
his prayer chapel filled with precious
donations and this had gone on for a while,

but then as a spectacle to the rabble
he had been roasted in Würzburg.
Already I can see, he resumed,
under the rainbow arching
over the land, the horsemen
advance from their camp.
Brothers, he said, when they were walking
along the Windsheim woods,
I know that the old coat is tearing
and I am afraid
of the ending of time.
In mid-May, when Grünewald
with his carved altarpiece had
returned to Frankfurt, the grain
whitening at harvest-time,
the whetted sickle passed
through the life of an army of five thousand
in the curious battle of Frankenhausen
in which hardly one horse soldier fell
but the bodies of peasants piled up
into a hecatomb, because,
as though they were mad,
they neither put up any resistance
nor took to their heels.
When Grünewald got news of this
on the 18th of May

he ceased to leave his house.
Yet he could hear the gouging out
of eyes that long continued
between Lake Constance and
the Thuringian Forest.
For weeks at that time he wore
a dark bandage over his face.

···VIII···

With the painter on horseback,
sometimes, too, high up on the cart
sits a nine-year-old child,
his own, as he ponders in disbelief,
conceived in his marriage to Anna.
It is a most beautiful ride, this last
in September 1527, along the riverside
through the valleys. The air stirs the light
between the leafage of trees, and from the hillsides
they look down on the land extending around them.
At rest, leaning against a rock, Grünewald
feels inside himself his misfortune
and that of the water artist in Halle.
The wind drives us into flight
like starlings at the hour when
the shadows fall. What remains to the last
is the work undertaken. In the service of
the family Erbach at Erbach, Grünewald devotes

the remaining years to an altar work.
Crucifixion again, and the lamentation,
the deformation of life slowly proceeds, and
always between the eye's glance
and the raising of his brush
Grünewald now covers a long journey,
much more often than he used to
interrupts the execution of his art
for the apprenticing of his child
both in the workplace and outside in the green country.
What he himself learned from this is nowhere reported,
only that the child at the age of fourteen
for no known reason suddenly died
and that the painter did not outlive him
for any great length of time. Peer ahead sharply,
there you see in the greying of nightfall
the distant windmills turn.
The forest recedes, truly,
so far that one cannot tell
where it once lay, and the ice-house
opens, and rime, on to the field, traces
a colourless image of Earth.
So, when the optic nerve
tears, in the still space of the air
all turns as white as
the snow on the Alps.

AND IF I REMAINED
BY THE OUTERMOST SEA

. . . Immer steigender hebst, Woge, du dich!
Ach! die letzte, letzte bist du! das Schiff geht unter!
Und den Todtengesang heult dumpf fort,
Auf dem großen, immer offenen Grabe der Sturm!

. . . Higher and higher, billow, you rise!
Ah, you're the last, the last! the ship's going down!
And muted, over the grave yet open and huge,
Still the gale howls its death-chant, its dirge.

Friedrich Gottlieb Klopstock, "The Worlds," Feb. 1746

··· I ···

Georg Wilhelm Steller
born at Windsheim, in Franconia,
while pursuing his studies
at the University of Halle
repeatedly came across news
items in journals
that the Russian Czarina,
in the course of her empire's expansion,
was preparing an expedition on an unprecedented scale
under the supreme command of Vitus Bering
to the Pacific coast, so that
the sea route from there to America
should become known.

.

··· II ···

Visions of this voyage of discovery,
Steller later recorded, had so seized
his imagination that he, the son
of a cantor, gifted with a
fine tenor voice and furnished
with a bursary for true Christians,
having abandoned Wittenberg and
theology for natural science,
could now, during his doctoral
disputations, which he passed
with the highest distinction,
think of nothing other than
the shapes of the fauna and
flora of that distant region
where East and West and North
converge, and of the art and skill
required for their description.

··· III ···

Although it was said that the authorities
would appoint him in the near future
to the Chair of Botany and so
accredit him to society,
Steller, without means though he was,
and with scarcely more than his notebooks
in his pocket, on the very day
after the Rigorosum set out in the
mail coach to the city of Danzig,
then occupied by Russian troops,
where he signed on as a medical assistant
on a packet-boat that was
to carry some hundreds
of invalids back to Russia.

··· IV ···

When the ship sailed out of Danzig Bay,
Steller, who had never yet confronted
the sea, stood on the deck for a while,
wondering at the passage
over water, at power and weight,
at the salt in the air and
the darkness pushed down to the deep
under the keel. To the left,
the outermost point of the Putzig spit,
to the right, the headland
fronting the Frische Haff,
a pale grey streak endlessly
merging into a still paler grey.
This behind him had been Germany,
it occurred to him, his childhood,
the woods of Windsheim;
the learning of ancient languages,
protracted throughout his youth

perscrutamini scripturas,

shouldn't that read,

perscrutamini naturas rerum?

...V...

Kronstadt, Oranienbaum, Peterhof
and last in the Torricellian void,
a thirty-four-year-old bastard,
marooned on the Neva's marsh delta,
St. Petersburg under the fortress,
the new Russian capital,
uncanny to a stranger,
no more than a chaos erupting,
buildings that began to subside
as soon as erected, and nowhere
a vista quite straight. The streets
and squares laid out according
to the Golden Section, jetty walls and bridges,
alignments, façades and rows of windows—
these only slowly come towards us
out of the future's resounding emptiness,
so as to bring the plan of eternity into the city
born of the terror of the vastness of space,

overpopulated with Armenians, Turks, Tatars,
Kalmucks, immigrant Swedes,
Germans, French and the tortured-to-death,
mutilated corpses of criminals hung
all down the avenue on exhibition.

··· VI ···

On the other side of the river, in the famous
botanical gardens of the Marine Hospital
Steller escapes the city's bustle.
Neatly he walks the paths
between the flowerbeds, marvels at
the hothouses, filled with tropical plants,
learns one new name after another
and is almost beside himself
with so much hope
when, from the half-shadow
of the mustard tree by the aviary,
the Patriarch of Novgorod,
Archbishop Theophon, steps towards him
with a tiny yellow parakeet in his hand,
and in the course of a Latin conversation
tells him a legend from the region of Dolyi,
which relates that God quite suddenly
and as though out of the blue came
into being on a lungwort leaf.

··· VII ···

For four years Steller remained
in Petersburg. The Primate, already
close to death, obtains for him the post
of an assistant in the Academy
and takes him into his own house
as a personal physician.
Under night's biretta the old man
talks with his younger brother
of the winged end. To comfort him
Steller speaks of the light of nature.
But all things, Theophon says,
all things, my son, transmute
into old age, life diminishes,
everything declines,
the proliferation
of kinds is a mere
illusion, and no one
knows to what end.

··· VIII ···

The long Arctic journeys
had frayed the nerves of the
Academy member Daniel Messerschmidt.
Steller, who found Messerschmidt still living
in the summerhouse he occupied
with a baker's daughter
from Sesslach, came too late
to get anything out of
the deeply melancholic man.
Instead, he now studies his papers.
He spends the whole summer
bent over the jumble of cards,
while the naturalist's neglected
wife, gaudily dressed, sits
beside him and with her split
fin strokes the glans that throbs
like his heart. Steller feels science
shrinking to a single slightly

painful point. On the other hand
the foam bubbles, to him, are
a paradigm. Come, he whispers
into her ear in his desperation,
come with me to Siberia as
my true wife, and already hears
the answer: wherever
you go I will
go with you.

···IX···

When in 1736 Steller did indeed
receive the longed-for appointment
to join the Bering expedition,
this enterprise, launched ten years previously,
consisting of an army of carpenters,
blacksmiths, grooms, mariners,
clerks, commissioned officers,
scientists and assistants,
and of not only building materials, tools, instruments,
an arsenal of weapons and many hundreds
of books, but also endless
forage trains for the team's provision,
crockery and clothing and crates
of claret for the higher-ranking
Academy emissaries, to be dragged onwards,
no different from a glacier pushing
great heavy masses of scree in its passage,
arrived at Yakutsk on the one hundred and
twenty-ninth degree of longitude, east.

Steller mastered the five thousand miles
in the course of the three and a half years
which Vitus Bering still needed
to convey everything, down to the last nail,
with his little Siberian packhorses
over the Yablonovy Range to
the Sea of Okhotsk. In the process
he accustomed himself to endure
deprivation and loneliness for
the sake of the baker's daughter,
whom, in the hope that
perhaps even in far-off places
one might feel at home and on the grounds
of her seemingly unconditional
promise to travel gladly with him
to any parts wheresoever, he'd made his wife,
but who in the end, naturally, had not been willing
to make that journey halfway round the globe
together with him. In place of her, Steller
now had two young ravens,
which in the evenings dictated
ominous sayings to him.
When he wrote these down
he felt some comfort, although he knew
that even with these he would not
arrest the slow corrosion
that had entered his soul.

··· X ···

On the twentieth of March, 1741,
Steller stepped into the long
blockhouse of the Petropavlovsk
command post on the eastern shore
of the Kamchatka Peninsula.
In a windowless recess, no larger
than six feet by six, at the far end
of the building's interior,
in no other way subdivided, he finds,
at a table of planks nailed together,
covered by land maps
and sea charts showing
vast tracts of whiteness,
Bering, the Commandant-captain,
his fifty-nine-year-old
head supported by his
right hand tattooed
with a bird's unfolded wings,

the left hand holding
a pair of dividers,
sitting motionless
in a flickering light.
It takes an uncannily
long time, Steller thinks,
for Bering to open
his eyes and look
at him. What is this
being called human?
A beast, shrouded
in deep mourning,
in a black coat
lined with
black fur.

For two weeks, with the wind fair,
the ships named after the saints
Peter and Paul had borne south
on the Arctic Ocean,
but the legendary land Gama entered
on Delisle's map nowhere emerged
from the water's waste. Only once on the
shimmering surface ahead did the watch
make out something black
covered with countless seabirds.
Plumbing the depth, they approached
till it was clear that the island rock
was no more than a dead whale many times magnified
by the mirage's play, adrift belly up.
After that the course was set
to north-northeast. In the nights,
at times the sea lit up,
and to the sails splattered

by the crests of waves
sparks of that light adhered.
In a second mirage
one evening, across the horizon's length
appeared a tract of land,
all crystalline marble,
but not until the morning of July 15th,
almost six weeks after setting sail
from the Bay of Avatsha,
did Steller, who always went on deck
in the early hours, truly see
between the low-drifting clouds
the feebly cross-hatched contour
of a mountain range.
In the evening of that day
the mist completely lifted.
A black sky
now overhung the sea and
the snow-covered, ragged merlons
of Alaska loomed "resplendent,"
the word that seemed right to Steller,
in rosy red and purple colours.
Vitus Bering, who throughout the voyage
had lain in his cabin staring
at the ceiling of beams above his head,
roused by the incessant jubilation

of the crew, for the first time came aloft

and contemplated the scene

in a fit of deepest depression.

··· XII ···

Unending flights
of screeching birds, which skimmed
low over the water,
from afar resembled
drifting islands. Whales
rotated around the ship, emitting
water-spouts high into the air
in all directions of the compass.
Chamisso, who later marvelled at
the same spectacular sight
on the Romanzov expedition,
was led to think that perhaps
these animals could be tamed
and—no different from geese
on a stubble field—be herded
with a rod, as it were, on the sea.
Bring up the young in a fjord, he wrote,
fasten a spiked belt buoyed up by

air-bladders under their pectoral fins,
let them unlearn their submersions,
make experiments. Whether the whale is
then to draw or to carry,
whether and how it is harnessed
or laden, how it is bridled
or otherwise governed, and who is to be the
mahout of this water-elephant—all this
will settle itself in time. Chamisso,
it is true, also writes
of the steam engine as
the first warm-blooded animal
created by humankind.

··· XIII ···

At the break of the following day,
St. Elijah's Day,
Steller went ashore. Ten hours
Bering, with dread already imprinted
on his brow, had granted him
for a scientific excursion.
Now a deep blueness
pervaded both water and the forests
that grew right down
to the coast. Unperturbed
animals came close to Steller, black
and red foxes, magpies too, jays and
crows went with him on his way
across the beach. In the translucent darkness
between the trees he moved
with a tread more like hovering
over a cushion of moss a foot thick.
He came close to simply proceeding

towards the mountains, into
cool wilderness, but the constructs
of science in his head,
directed towards a diminution
of disorder in our world,
ran counter to that need.
Later, in a shelter made
out of joined fir-logs, he experienced
the effect of forsaken things
in a foreign space. A circular
drinking vessel of peeled-off bark,
a whetstone dotted with copper ore,
a fish-head paddle and
a child's rattle of fired clay
he carefully selects, and in their place
leaves behind an iron kettle, a string
of many-coloured beads,
a little strip of Bokhara silk,
half a pound of tobacco and
a Chinese clay pipe.
After half a century this mute
exchange is still remembered,
as can be seen in a report by Commander Billings,
by an inhabitant of this remote region
with a laugh that's a rustling
turned inwards.

··· XIV ···

The advice of the officers was
to make for Avatsha, keeping the course
as close as practicable to the fifty-third parallel
after the unanimous decision
to forgo any further exploration,
a simple calculation that rested
on nothing but unknown factors.
For almost a quarter of a year
the ship was tossed hither and thither
by hurricanes of a force
none in the team could recall
ever having experienced, on the Bering Sea
where there was nothing and no one but them.
All was a greyness, without direction,
with no above or below, nature
in a process of dissolution, in a state
of pure dementia. For days, in between
lulls, the ship motionless and

ever more and more damaged,
more tattered, the rigging more threadbare,
the sailcloth eaten away by salt.
The crew, stricken with
the delirium that comes of diseases
that entered their bodies, with eyes
drowning in exhaustion,
gums swollen like sponges,
joints suffused with blood,
liver puffed up, spleen puffed up
and with ulcers festering
just under the skin, day after day in God's name
flung overboard sailors rotted away, till at last
there was scarcely a difference between
the living and the dead.
In dying the astra in human bodies
lose their quality, kind, substance
and essence, Steller, the physician, thinks,
what is dead has ceased to be living.
What does it mean, this *physica,* he asks,
what this *iusiurandum Hippocratis,*
what does *surgery* mean, what is our
skill and use when life
breaks apart and the physician
has neither might nor means? There—
in the night—with the moon

in its first November quarter,
a great wall of water drives
the ship onto the rocks.
Jammed there it lies, groans
for a while amid boulders
as though in its last extremity
it might yet reach dry land,
until a heavy wave
pushes it down into the stillness
of the lagoon behind the reef.
A white sickle the strand
curves in the dark, inland
the dunes overgrown with grasses
up to a plateau of shadows
under mountains in snowlight,
phosphorescent.

··· XV ···

Four men carried Bering, when inch by inch
water had risen right into him,
on to land on a seat of ropes tied together,
leaned him against a rock that broke the wind's
fury and made a roof out of the sails
of the *St. Peter*. Wrapped in greatcoats, furs
and cloaks, his face yellow-wrinkled, his mouth
toothless, a black ruin, plagued with boils and
lice all over his body, the captain observed,
full of contentment in the face of death,
the first labours towards the erection
of winter quarters in the lairs
of foxes dug in the dunes.
Steller brings Bering a soup
concocted of blubber and nasturtium roots
which, however, turning his head aside,
Bering refuses
with a blink of his eyes.

Let them now, he says,
just leave him to sink
into the sand. The wrens
are already hopping about on him.
Blessed are the dead, Steller
remembers. On December 8th
they tie the captain on to a plank
and push him down into the hole.
It is not Thy will, Lord, to abandon
to the wild beasts the souls
of them that profess Thee.
Rather for the faithful a meal shall
be prepared from Leviathan's heart.
Steller, looking up, sees
the greenish-grey reflex from the ocean,
the Arctic water-sky,
under the clouds. A sign of
how far they still are
from land.

···XVI···

On August 13th
the ship built from the wreck
sails round the island's outermost
promontory which with gentle hills and calm
outlines descends to the sea.
Glistening in lovely greenness
like the pasture slopes of the Alps
it lies in late summer's light,
untouched, it seems, by man.
Seen from on board,
the land moves.
Time past
grows no more real
through sufferings endured.
Incomprehensible, too, on the horizon
above the blue
vapour spread over the land,
after four days at sea

the smoke trails from Asia's volcanoes.
To get close to this vista
they tack beneath the coast,
at one-quarter of a knot per hour
southward a good week long,
by night pull at the oars, too,
until, on the twenty-fifth of the month,
they reach the harbour of Petropavlovsk,
its plundered blockhouses and stores.
In thanksgiving for the miracle of their release
and in accordance with Bering's wish
they make a silver frame,
beaten out of the coins, left unspent
to the last, for St. Peter's icon.

···XVII···

Six years went by
before the survivors of the expedition
received the order
to return to the capital.
But Steller a few days after their landfall
in the Bay of Avatsha
had detached himself from the corps
and with the Cossack Lepekhin
had set out on foot for the peninsula's interior.
If it please Thee that we travel,
so in his mind he said, be Thou
our strength as we go,
our comfort on the way, shade
in the heat of noon,
light in darkness,
shelter from frost and rain,
conveyance at the hour of weariness,
help in extremity, so that

under Thy guidance
safely we may attain that place
to which we are drawn;
Thine be the care, Lord,
so that the stars propitiously
conjoin above us.

···XVIII···

During what remained of the summer
Steller collects botanical specimens,
fills little bags with dried seed,
describes, classifies, draws,
sits in his black travelling tent,
happy for the first time in his life.
Thoma Lepekhin catches salmon,
brings mushrooms, berries and leaves,
makes fire and tea.
Throughout the winter
the German doctor teaches
Koryak children in a tiny
wooden school, writes
when the ice breaks
memoranda in defence
of the indigenous people maltreated
and deprived of their rights by
the Naval Command at Bolsheretsk—
with the consequence that a letter against him

is despatched, that interrogations take place,
that misunderstandings arise,
that arrests follow and that Steller
now wholly grasps the difference
between nature and society.
Westward, stage after stage he covers
fleeing back, and it seems as though
everything now were going downhill.
Only in Tara does the message reach him
that by any route possible
he may now set out for his home.
Steller hires three horses,
drives to Tobolsk,
and there he,
who never drank, drinks
for three whole days.
Then comes the fever,
he creeps into the sledge,
tells the Tatar to drive on southward,
the hundred and seventy miles to Tyumen.
This is *infirmitas,* the breaking
of time from day to day
and from hour to hour,
it is rust and fire
and the salt of the planets
darkness even at noon and
luminaries absent from heaven.

··· XIX ···

Manuscripts written at the end of his life,
on an island in the glacial sea,
with scratching goose-quill in bilious ink,
lists of two hundred and eleven
different plants, tales of white ravens,
unknown cormorants and sea-cows,
gathered into the dust
of an endless inventory,
his zoological masterpiece
De Bestiis Marinis,
travel chart for hunters,
blueprint for the counting of pelts—
no, not steep enough
was the north.

··· XX ···

At Tyumen they carry him out of the sledge,
drag his half-petrified body
out of the ice into the fire,
into a furnace house.
Now begins *alchimia,*
Steller recognises the *mortem improvisam,*
the stroke and all its appendage,
sees his death, how it is mirrored
in the field-surgeon's monocle.
Such are you, *doctores,*
spilt lamps,
thus nature has her way
with a godless
Lutheran from Germany.

··· XXI ···

Pallas tells how Steller, whom he revered,
the next day,
wrapped in his red cloak,
a good distance outside the place of rest
of the believers was laid in a narrow ditch
high up above the Tura's banks,
how they heaped up a mound
of frozen sods. Pallas
writes too that the dead man
was dreaming still of the grazing
mammoth across the river
until in the night someone came
and took his cloak
and left him to lie in the snow
like a fox beaten to death.

DARK NIGHT SALLIES FORTH

et iam summa procul villarum culmina fumant
maioresque cadunt altis de montibus umbrae

and now far-off smoke pearls from homestead rooftops
and from high mountains the greater shadows fall

Virgil, *Eclogues* I

···I···

For it is hard to discover
the winged vertebrates of prehistory
embedded in tablets of slate.
But if I see before me
the nervature of past life
in one image, I always think
that this has something to do
with truth. Our brains, after all,
are always at work on some quivers
of self-organisation, however faint,
and it is from this that an order
arises, in places beautiful
and comforting, though more cruel, too,
than the previous state of ignorance.
How far, in any case, must one go back
to find the beginning? Perhaps
to that morning of January 9th, 1905,
on which Grandfather and Grandmother

in ringing cold drove in an open
landau from Kloster Lechfeld
to Obermeitingen, to be married.
Grandmother in a black taffeta dress
with a bunch of paper flowers, Grandfather
in his uniform, the brass-embellished
helmet on his head. What was in their minds
when, the horse blanket over their knees,
they sat side by side in the carriage and
heard the hoofbeats echo
in the bare avenue?
What was in the minds
of their children later, one of whom
stares out fearfully from
a class photograph taken
in the war year 1917
at Allarzried? Forty-eight
pitiable coevals,
the schoolmistress on the right,
on the left the myopic
chaplain and as a caption
on the reverse of the
spotted grey cardboard mount
the words "in the future
death lies at our feet,"
one of those obscure oracular sayings

one never again forgets. On another
photograph of which I possess an enlarged
copy, a swan and its reflection
on the water's black surface,
a perfect emblem of peace.
The botanical garden around the pond,
to my knowledge, is situated
on the bank of the Regnitz at Bamberg
and I believe that a road
runs through it today.
The whole leaves an impression
that is somehow un-German,
the elms, the hornbeams and densely green
conifers in the background, the small
pagoda-like building, the finely raked
gravel, the hortensias, flag-iris,
aloes, ostrich-plume ferns and
the giant-leaved ornamental rhubarb.
Astonishing, to me, the persons
also to be seen in the picture:
Mother in her open coat,
with a lightness she was
later to lose; Father,
a little aside, hands in his pockets,
he too, it seems, with no cares.
The date is August 26th, 1943.

On the 27th Father's departure for Dresden,
of whose beauty his memory, as he
remarks when I question him,
retains no trace.
During the night of the 28th
582 aircraft flew in
to attack Nürnberg. Mother,
who on the next day planned
to return to her parents'
home in the Alps,
got no further than
Fürth. From there she
saw Nürnberg in flames,
but cannot recall now
what the burning town looked like
or what her feelings were
at this sight.
On the same day, she told me recently,
from Fürth she had travelled on
to Windsheim and an acquaintance
at whose house she waited until
the worst was over, and realized
that she was with child.
As for the burning city,
in the Vienna Art-Historical Museum
there hangs a painting

by Altdorfer depicting Lot
with his daughters. On the horizon
a terrible conflagration blazes
devouring a large city.
Smoke ascends from the site,
the flames rise to the sky and
in the blood-red reflection
one sees the blackened
façades of houses.
In the middle ground there is a strip
of idyllic green landscape,
and closest to the beholder's eye
the new generation of
Moabites is conceived.
When for the first time I saw
this picture the year before last,
I had the strange feeling
of having seen all of it
before, and a little later,
crossing to Floridsdorf
on the Bridge of Peace,
I nearly went out of my mind.

At the moment on Ascension Day
of the year 'forty-four when I was born,
the procession for the blessing of the fields
was just passing our house to the sounds
of the fire brigade band, on its way out
to the flowering May meadows. Mother
at first took this as a happy sign, unaware
that the cold planet Saturn ruled this hour's
constellation and that above the mountains
already the storm was hanging which soon thereafter
dispersed the supplicants and killed
one of the four canopy bearers.
Apart from the grievous impression this
occurrence, unprecedented in the village's history,
may have made upon me, and apart from
the raging fire which one night—shortly
before my first day at school it was—
consumed a sawmill not far from our house

and lit up the whole valley, I grew up,
despite the dreadful course
of events elsewhere, on the northern
edge of the Alps, so it seems
to me now, without any
idea of destruction. But the habit
of often falling down in the street and
often sitting with bandaged hands
by the open window between the potted
fuchsias, waiting for the
pain to subside and for hours
doing nothing but looking out,
early on induced me to imagine
a silent catastrophe that occurs
almost unperceived.
What I thought up at the time,
while gazing down into the herb garden
in which the nuns under their white
starched hoods moved so slowly
between the beds as though a moment ago
they had still been caterpillars, this
I have never got over.
The emblem for me of the
scarcely identifiable disaster
since that time has been a stunted
Tatar with a red headcloth

and a white slightly curved
feather. In anthropology
this figure is often associated
with certain forms of self-mutilation
and described as that of the adept who
ascends a snow-covered mountain and long
tarries there, as they say, in tears.
In a sheltered corner
of his heart, so lately
I have read, he carries
a little horse made
of clay. Magical
crosswords he mumbles,
talks of scissor blades,
a thimble, a needle's
eye, a stone in the memory,
a place of pilgrimage, and
of a small die, ice-coloured,
with a dash of Berlin blue.
A long series of tiny shocks,
from the first and the second pasts,
not translated into the spoken
language of the present, they
remain a broken corpus guarded
by Fungisi and the wolf's shadow.
After that come the children grown

a little bigger who believe that
parts of their parents ride ahead
on the removal van's horse
to make ready the living quarters,
while in the dark box
on the way to Gmunden
they eat their supper,
drink two pots of coffee,
spread butter on the bread
and say not a word about
either herring or radish. For months
Grandmother's dying has now dragged on,
more and more water rising into her body
while in the village shop a poster
outlaws the yellowing
terror of Colorado beetles.
At the forest's edge often a blackamoor
peered out of an American tank
and in the dark we saw
St. Elizabeth, lifting her skirts,
cautiously stepping over
red-hot ploughshares.
At school the beadle counted
his keys, Palm Sunday catkins
behind the crucifix chanted
their credo, and in the pencil case

on a scrap of paper already
the catchword of our dusty
future could be made out.
So one of us turned
into an innkeeper, the second
into a cook, the third into a waiter and
the fourth into nothing at all.
And from the hills we can see
the wispy shadows drifting
in Jehoshaphat's Valley.
The magnetic needle, trembling,
points to the north, and I sense
a galvanic taste on my tongue,
a chemical miracle plated inside
with the finest horn silver.
The dreaded blackening
on certain parts
of the body confirms
the whole thing
most satisfactorily.

··· III ···

In a Chinese cricket cage
for a time we kept good fortune
imprisoned. The Paradise apples
grew splendidly, a good mass of gold
lay on the barn floor and you said,
one must watch over the
bridegroom as over a
scholar by night. Often
it was carnival time
for the children. Pink
cloudlets hung in the
sky. Friends came
disguised as Ormuzd
and Ahriman. But then unexpectedly
there was this thing with the elegant
gentleman at the opera and I found
a slowworm in the henhouse.
A crow on the wing lost a white

feather. The vicar, a limping
messenger in a black coat,
appeared on New Year's morning
alone on the wide snow-covered field.
Ever since we've been arming ourselves
with patience, ever since sand
has been trickling through the letter box,
the potted plants have had a way of
keeping things to themselves.
A Nordic tragedy, chess
pieces moved hither and
thither, inevitably always
the end occurs. Why
do we embark on such
an arduous enterprise?
For comfort there remains
nothing but other people's
misfortune: a feather
venomously yellow
on the beloved's hat.
Prose from the last century,
a dress entangled in
thistles, a bit of blood,
an exaltation, a torn-up letter,
a star on the uniform and prolonged
stays at the window. Unhealthy

fantasies in a darkening
room, resented sins,
yes, even tears and in the memory
of fishes a dying fire, Emma,
how she burns the wedding bouquet.
What's a poor country doctor
to make of all that? At the funeral
he dreams of a shining pair of
patent-leather boots and a posthumous
seduction. But now comes
a colourless age. You, in the midst
of this dazzling obscenity
I shall remember your
timorous gaze, how I
saw it first, that time
when in Haarlem we swam
through a gap in the dike.
Anniversaries and numbers,
how long ago it all is,
a chart of signs barely
to be deciphered through
these glass lenses. I still
can hear the Chinese lady
optician say, You ought
now to be able to read this
without straining your eyes,

and for a moment I feel
her fingertips on my temples,
feel how a wave crosses
my heart and in the test picture's
bright square I see
the letter sequence
YAMOUSSOUKRO,
the name, I am
certain of this,
of a large rusty ship
from Abidjan which years ago
I saw putting out from
Hamburg harbour.
Black sailors stood
leaning on the rails,
they waved to us as they
passed by, the sun was just
going down and already
the shadows were quivering
at the edges.

···IV···

In his excitement about the truly
boundless growth
of industry, the statesman
Disraeli called Manchester
the most wonderful city of modern times,
a celestial Jerusalem
whose significance only philosophy
could gauge. Half a life ago now
it is that, after leaving my remote home,
I arrived there and took lodging
among the previous century's
ruins. Often at that time
I rambled over the fallow
Elysian Fields, wondering
at the work of destruction, the black
mills and shipping canals,
the disused viaducts and
warehouses, the many millions

of bricks, the traces of smoke,
of tar and sulphuric acid,
long have I stood on the banks
of the Irk and the Irwell, those
mythical rivers now dead,
which in better times
shone azure-blue,
carmine-red and glaucous green,
in their glow reflecting
the cotton clouds, those white ones
into which without a word the breath
of legions of human beings had been absorbed.
And the water carried them downstream
together with salt and ashes
through the marshland out
to the sea. Those silent mutations
clear the way to the future.
In the course of three generations
the working classes of Manchester
had become a race of pygmies.
Volunteers who in war-time attempted
to escape into military service
were rejected by the selection boards
as unfit, unless they could be accommodated
in one of the so-called bantam battalions
which recruited diminutive soldiers from the city

and throughout the surrounding area.
In either case they were
part of the obscure crowds
who fuelled the progress of history.
From my workplace I thought
I could see the will-o'-the-wisps
of their souls, as with tiny lanterns
they haunted the rubbish dumps
of the City Corporation, a smouldering
alpine range which, it seemed to me,
extended into the beyond.
In the dusk I often saw
searchlight beams from
bulldozers creeping about there
that pierced the void, and aeroplanes,
our grey primeval brothers,
rose with infinite slowness
from the lagoon and the bogs.
I recall that these images
often plunged me into a quasi
sublunary state of deep
melancholia and that then
I heard the incessant monotonous
vibrations of a Jew's harp
and repeatedly had to step out
of doors in my oppression.

Whole days long in the basement
of the university library I read
the works of Paracelsus, in which
it is written that from septentrion
nothing good emanates and
that the body is dyed
by illness like a piece of cloth
by an extraneous colour.
Often on my wanderings
through the streets I resorted
to one of the many infernally
glittering hostelries, for preference
to Liston's Music Hall
where a radiantly blue-eyed,
down-and-out heroic tenor,
who always wore a winter coat
too long for him and a Homburg hat,
sang *Tannhäuser* arias accompanied
by a Wurlitzer organ. And to
the Gospel Chapels I went
from time to time, witnessing
how row after row of the sick
amid the congregation's shrieking
were healed and even the blind
had their sight restored.
Once, while searching

for the star-shaped Strangeways
Prison, an overwhelming
panoptic structure whose walls
are as high as Jericho's, I found
myself in a sort of no-man's-land
behind the railway buildings, in a terrace
of low houses apparently due
for demolition, with shops left vacant,
on whose boards the names
Goldblatt, Grünspan and Gottgetreu,
Spiegelhalter, Solomon, Waislfish
and Robinsohn could be made out.
In the wind a door moved
as if as a sign. Stuck to it
was an old placard
for the musical *Oklahoma!*
The entrance to nature's theatre
stood open. I still strained
to hear the ethereal waves
when with martial brass music,
bugle horns and drums,
a procession of olive-green
child soldiers marched
down the street, passed
by me and suddenly vanished
as though swallowed by the earth.

If I told Mr. Deutsch
about these things
he shook his head
and said: "Strange, very
strange." Mr. Deutsch,
born in Kufstein, had come
to England as a child
in nineteen thirty-eight.
There were many things he could not
remember; some others he could not erase
from his mind. He had never
mastered the English language
although for years, day in
and day out, he followed
on TV with an expression of
the utmost attention the entire
evening schedule, as if
at any moment he expected
a message that would
change his whole life.

···V···

When, in the summer of last year,
I visited the engineer D. in Zürich
he was sitting by an open window
and kept turning a piece of feldspar
around in his hands. You see,
he said, outside, the garden grows rank,
my place now is in the midst of the foliage.
That reminds me of the migration
through the desert. How many machines
I'd built, how many works designed,
before I lost my belief
in the science I'd always served.
I had arrived at one of the dead
bays of time, like that Tatar
with the red headcloth and the white
curved feather, had climbed the mountain
and surveyed the city, as it lay
before me, a faded picture

of the great *diluvium.*
I sensed the trembling
of the aerials on the roofs
of houses as a frizzle
in my brain, could hear from far away
outside me
the Gaussian roar, an unremitting
sound extending over the whole scale
from the earth up to the heavens
where the stars drift
in the aether. Many
terrible midnights
of doubt have I passed
since that time, but now peace
returns to the dust and I read
in the descriptions of nature
of the eighteenth century how a
verdant land is submerged
in the blue shadows of the Jurassus
and in the end only the age-old
ice on the Alps retains a faint
afterglow. A strange light pervades
the lines of Haller and Hölderlin
and yet even here there is vagary
as far as the heart reaches. For
the revolutions of great
systems cannot be

righted, too diffuse are
the workings of power
the one thing always
the other's beginning
and vice versa. *Taurus*
draconem genuit et draco
taurum, and nowhere
a stop. So you'd better be off,
said the engineer D., this very day.
The country's on fire already and everywhere
the forests are ablaze, there's a crackling
of fire in the fanned leaves
and the drought-stricken African
plains are expanding. Still
perhaps on your travels
you'll see a golden coast
a land veneered with rain or
a schoolboy on his way home
over a beautiful meadow. Then
another joy will have been lived,
thinks one who recovers a little.
The shady shore of a lake
emerges, the water's surface,
the ribbons of rocks and
on the highest summit the dragon's
many-coloured plumage, Icarus,
sailing in the midst of

the currents of light. Beneath him
time divides the Rhine glacier
into two mighty branches,
the Churfirsten peaks emerge,
the Säntis range rises,
chalk islets, glowing
bright in drifting ice.
If his eyes are now
lowered, if he falls
down into the lake,
will then, as in Brueghel's
picture, the beautiful ship,
the ploughing peasant, the whole
of nature somehow turn away
from the son's misfortune?
These questions carry me
over the border. On the Arlberg
a thunderstorm gathers.
I gaze down into the valley
and my soul is sent reeling.
Another summer gone by and
as ivy hangs down, Hölderlin wrote,
so does branchless the rain. Moss roses
grow on the Alps. Avignon sylvan.
Across the Gotthard a horse gropes its way.

··· VI ···

When morning sets in,
the coolness of night
moves out into the plumage
of fishes, when once more
the air's circumference
grows visible, then at times
I trust the quiet, resolve
to make a new start, an excursion
perhaps to a reserve of
camouflaged ornithologists.
Come, my daughter, come on,
give me your hand, we're leaving
the town, I'll show you the mill
set twice each day in motion
by the sea's current,
a groaning miraculous construct
of wheels and belts
that carries water power

right into stone, right
into the trickling dust and
into the bodies of spiders.
The miller is friendly,
has clean white paws,
tells us all kinds of lore
to do with the story of flour.
A century ago Edward FitzGerald,
the translator of Omar Khayyám,
vanished out there. At an advanced age
one day he boarded his boat,
sailed off, with his top hat
tied on, into the German ocean
and was never seen again.
A great enigma, my child,
look, here are eleven barrows
for the dead and in the sixth
the impress of a ship with forty oars
long since gone, the grave of
Raedwald of Sutton Hoo.
Merovingian coins, Swedish
armour, Byzantine silver
the king took on his voyage,
and his warriors even now
on this sandy strip keep their weapons
hidden in grassy bunkers

behind earthworks, barbed wire
and pine plantations, one great
arsenal as far as your eye can see,
and nothing else but this sky,
the gorse scrub and now and then,
an old people's home,
a prison or an asylum,
an institution for juvenile delinquents.
In orange jackets you see
the inmates labour
lined up across the moor.
Behind that the end
of the world, the five
cold houses of Shingle Street.
Inconsolable a woman
stands at the window,
a children's swing
rusts in the wind, a lonely
spy sits in his Dormobile
in the dunes, his headphones
pulled over his ears.
No, here we can write
no postcards, can't even
get out of the car. Tell me, child,
is your heart as heavy as
mine is, year after year

a pebble bank raised
by the waves of the sea
all the way to the North,
every stone a dead soul
and this sky so grey?
So unremittingly grey
and so low as no sky
I have seen before.
Along the horizon
freighters cross over
into another age
measured by the ticking
of Geigers in the power station
at Sizewell, where slowly
the core of the metal
is destroyed. Whispering
madness on the heathland
of Suffolk. Is this
the promis'd end? Oh,
you are men of stones.
What's dead is gone
forever. What did'st
thou say? What,
how, where, when?
Is this love
nothing now

or all?

Water? Fire? Good?

Evil? Life? Death?

···VII···

Lord, I dreamed
that to see Alexander's battle
I flew all the way to
Munich. It was when darkness
crept in and far below me
I saw the roof of my house,
saw the shadows falling
on the East Anglian landscape,
I saw the rim of the island,
the waves lapping the shore
and in the North Sea the ships
motionless ahead of the foam-white wakes.
As a stingray hovers deep down
in the sea, so soundlessly I glided,
scarcely moving a wing,
high above the earth
over the Rhine's alluvial plain
and followed upstream

the course of the water
grown heavy and bitter.
Cities phosphorescent
on the riverbank, industry's
glowing piles waiting
beneath the smoke trails
like ocean giants for the siren's
blare, the twitching lights
of rail- and motorways, the murmur
of the millionfold proliferating molluscs,
wood lice and leeches, the cold putrefaction,
the groans in the rocky ribs,
the mercury shine, the clouds that
chased through the towers of Frankfurt,
time stretched out and time speeded up,
all this raced through my mind
and was already so near the end
that every breath of air made my
face shudder. A high surf,
the mountain oaks roared on the slopes
of the Odenwald and then came a desert
and waste through whose valleys
the wind drove the dust
of stones. A twice-honed
sword divided the sky
from the earth, an effulgence flowed

into space, and the destination
of my excursion, the vision
of Altdorfer, opened up.
Far more than one hundred thousand,
so the inscriptions proclaim,
number the dead over whom
the battle surges for the salvation
of the Occident in the rays
of a setting sun. This is
the moment when destiny turns.
At the centre of the grandiose thronging
of banners and flags, lances and
pikes and batons, the breastplated
bodies of human beings and animals,
Alexander, the western world's
hero, on his white horse
and before him in flight
towards the sickle moon
Darius, stark terror
visible in his face. As fortunate,
did the clever chaplain, who
had hung up an oleograph
of the battle scene beside
the blackboard describe the outcome
of this affair. It was,
he said, a demonstration

of the necessary destruction of all
the hordes coming up from the East,
and thus a contribution to the history
of salvation. Since then I have
read in another teacher's writings
that we have death in front of us
rather like a picture of Alexander's battle
on our schoolroom wall.
Now I know, as with a crane's eye
one surveys his far-flung realm,
a truly Asiatic spectacle,
and slowly learns, from the tininess
of the figures and the incomprehensible
beauty of nature that vaults over them
to see that side of life that
one could not see before. We look
over the battle and, glancing
from north to south, we see
a camp with white Persian
tents lying in the evening glow
and a city on the shore.
Outside, with swollen sails
the ships make headway and
the shadows already graze
the cypresses, and beyond them
Egypt's mainland extends.

The Nile Delta can be made out,
the Sinai Peninsula, the Red Sea
and, still farther in the distance,
towering up in dwindling light,
the mountain ranges,
snow-covered and ice-bound,
of the strange, unexplored,
African continent.

PUBLISHER'S NOTE

This translation of *After Nature* is published posthumously. W. G. Sebald approved a final version of the text before his death.

ABOUT THE AUTHOR

W. G. SEBALD was born in Wertach im Allgäu, Germany, in 1944. He studied German language and literature at Freiburg, Switzerland, and Manchester. He taught at the University of East Anglia in Norwich, England, for thirty years, becoming professor of European literature in 1987, and from 1989 to 1994 was the first director of the British Centre for Literary Translation. His books have won a number of international awards, including the National Book Critics Circle Award, the *Los Angeles Times* Book Award, the Berlin Literature Prize, and the Literatur Nord Prize. He died in December 2001.

ABOUT THE TRANSLATOR

MICHAEL HAMBURGER has written, translated, and edited across the fields of German, French, and Italian literature. He has held visiting posts at universities and colleges in America and Great Britain and has received many awards and honors, including two honorary doctorates, several prizes for his translations and, in 1992, an OBE. He has produced poetry throughout his writing life; his *Collected Poems 1941–1994* appeared in 1995 and his latest volume, *Intersections,* in 2000. His critical work on the subject, *The Truth of Poetry,* was published in 1972 by Penguin. He has also written his memoirs, *String of Beginnings* (1991).

A B O U T   T H E   T Y P E

This book was set in Perpetua, a typeface designed by the English artist Eric Gill, and cut by the Monotype Corporation between 1928 and 1930. Perpetua is a contemporary face of original design, without any direct historical antecedents. The shapes of the roman letters are derived from the techniques of stonecutting. The larger display sizes are extremely elegant and form a most distinguished series of inscriptional letters.

Printed in the United States
by Baker & Taylor Publisher Services